3-2-1
Time for Parachute Fun!

Clare Beswick

With contributions from:
Sandra Suffoletto Ryan, Buffalo, NY
Jenifer Galvin, Corvallis, OR
Judy Fujawa, The Villages, FL
Andrea Hungerford, Plainville, CT

3·2·1: Time for Parachute Fun

Clare Beswick

Illustrated by Jane Dippold

Copyright © 2010 Clare Beswick
Published by Gryphon House, Inc.
10770 Columbia Pike, Suite 201, Silver Spring, MD 20901
800.638.0928; 301.595.9500; 301.595.0051 (fax)

Visit us on the web at www.gryphonhouse.com

Illustrations: Jane Dippold

Library of Congress Cataloging-in-Publication Data

Beswick, Clare.
  3-2-1 : time for parachute fun! / by Clare Beswick ; with contributions
from Sandra Suffoletto Ryan ... [et al.] ; illustrated by Jane Dippold.
      p. cm.
  Includes index.
  ISBN 978-0-87659-300-4
  1. Early childhood education--Activity programs. 2. Creative activities and seat work. 3. Play. I. Dippold, Jane. II. Title.
  LB1139.35.A37B47 2010
  649'.51--dc22

                                                            2010001653

Text © Clare Beswick 2003
Originally published by Featherstone Education Ltd, 2003

Bulk purchase
Gryphon House books are available for special premiums and sales promotions as well as for fundraising use. Special editions or book excerpts also can be created to specification. For details, contact the Director of Marketing at Gryphon House.

Disclaimer
Gryphon House, Inc. and the authors cannot be held responsible for damage, mishap, or injury incurred during the use of or because of activities in this book. Appropriate and reasonable caution and adult supervision of children involved in activities and corresponding to the age and capability of each child involved is recommended at all times. Do not leave children unattended at any time. Observe safety and caution at all times.

Contents

5

Introduction

A parachute is a wonderful resource that you can use every day!

Although you may think that a parachute is most suited for promoting physical development, it is also a great way to develop social and emotional skills. In fact, a parachute can be used to promote active play, support imaginative play and creativity, improve listening and attention skills, develop an understanding of mathematical ideas and concepts, support communication and literacy skills, and much more.

This book provides a wealth of activities and play ideas that are easy to do, using a parachute and everyday materials. Teachers, family members, caregivers, and anyone working with children ages 3–10 will find the ideas in this book fun and educational.

Each activity has step-by-step instructions, including key words that you can use as the children play and learn with a parachute. Many activities offer additional ideas, providing plenty of inspiration to support children's learning. Most ideas can be adapted for children at different developmental stages or for multi-age groups.

Safety Tips for Parachute Play

- Choose the area for play carefully. The surface should be clean and smooth because many parachute activities involve crawling, kneeling, and sitting on the floor.
- Make sure that there is enough open space, and that no obstacles are around the parachute.
- Make sure children are dressed appropriately for active play.
- Keep the room cool or play outside on a cool day. Children can become hot during parachute play.
- Plan the parachute play session so that it flows smoothly, making the activity easy to understand.
- Start each session with a reminder of how to play safely.
- Keep your instructions short, clear, and easy to follow.

Parachute rules may include the following:

- Listen carefully.
- Stop when asked.
- Stop if the person next to you falls.
- Take care not to bump into others.

Do not allow children to play with a parachute without direct adult supervision. Young children may become entangled in the parachute. There is also a risk of suffocation.

Consider ending each parachute game by asking the children to perform one of these calming activities:

- Sit on the edge of the parachute and pass a handshake around the circle.
- Lie very still under the parachute while the adults waft the parachute gently up and down.
- Sit around the edge of the parachute with their eyes closed while they listen for their names to be called so they may move to the next activity.

3–2–1: Time for Parachute Fun!

- Walk around the parachute while holding it at waist height, gradually moving more slowly until they stop and gently rest the parachute on the floor.
- Lie down on the parachute and listen to some gentle music.

Thinking of Buying a Parachute?

Here are a few things to consider:

1. To determine which size parachute to buy, decide where you are going to use it and measure the smallest of these spaces. You will need plenty of space around the parachute that is free of obstacles and potential hazards.
2. Look for a parachute that is made of a strong but lightweight fabric.
3. Check that the seams of the parachute are sewn securely. They need to be strong enough to take plenty of active play.
4. Ask if you can specify the colors when you order. If you have a child with a visual impairment, consider purchasing a parachute made with bright- or fluorescent-colored sections.
5. Think about how you want to use the parachute. Use may influence your choice of design and size.

Note: For many of the games you can improvise with a large flat sheet, but to make the most of the activities and ideas, it is best to use a parachute. If you do not have a parachute, consider making one.

Using a Parachute Every Day

Aside from using a parachute every day to teach children certain skills and topics, you can use it to define new and interesting play areas and as a part of displays. Use the following ideas or make up your own:

- Attach a hook firmly to the ceiling of your room. Make sure the hook will hold the weight of all or most of the parachute.
- If your parachute has a hole in the middle, hook this opening over the ceiling hook. If your parachute does not have a hole in the middle, gather some of the parachute material from the center of the parachute (or, depending on what you want to create, from another part of the parachute) and wrap a strong cord around the material. Tie the cord so a loop remains and hang the loop onto the hook in the ceiling.

- Use the parachute to create a special imaginative play area in the room. Try using it as

  - a tent or big top for circus performers,
  - a tent for camping holidays,
  - the sails of a ship,
  - a restaurant,
  - the inside of the space shuttle, or
  - a jungle.

- Hang your parachute from a hook, as described above, or drape it (folded or opened fully) over furniture to create a special place, such as defining new areas where children

  - use real and improvised musical instruments;
  - rest and relax with story tapes, books, and soft toys; or
  - hear a special story.

- Use your parachute to spotlight or revive an area or brighten an existing area with a parachute backdrop.

- Make the entrance to a room special by draping a parachute over it. Leave plenty of headroom for adults to walk safely under the parachute's folds.

Remember: Make sure the parachute is fixed securely at all times; think ahead to avoid potential accidents.

Ideas to Add More Fun to Parachute Play

- Attach fabric letters, numbers, or shapes with Velcro to each color triangle of the parachute.
- Add small bells to the outside edge of the parachute.
- Trim the chute with different textured ribbons.
- Line the parachute with black fabric and use Velcro to attach fabric stars.

- Add some loops to the edge of parachute to make it easier for children to hold onto it.

- Make a huge parachute (about five yards in diameter) for parachute play in large areas. (You will need the help of several adults to play with a parachute of this size.)

- Try some of the parachute games with long narrow lengths of fabric, about one yard wide and five yards long.

Parachute Games—No Props Necessary

Parachute Play— The Basics

What You Need

▶ just a parachute

Sing familiar songs as you teach children how to use a parachute. Create a new song by changing a few of the words to make it fit the activity.

Vocabulary

- action
- billow
- circle
- edge
- grip
- hold on
- let go
- listen
- mushroom
- next
- practice
- round
- share
- together
- turn
- verse
- waft

What Children Learn

- To interact with others and work together toward a common goal
- To listen with enjoyment and respond to stories, songs and other music, and rhymes and poems
- To be confident about trying new activities

What to Do

1. Spread the parachute flat on the floor and sit around the edge with the children. Talk about all of the things one can do with a parachute. Explain that if the children hold a section of the chute and cooperate as a group, they will be able to move the parachute up, down, and all around.

2. Ask the children to take hold of the section of the parachute that is directly in front of them. Show them how to hold the material correctly by bunching it into each hand for a firm grip or by grabbing a handle if the parachute has handles.

3. Tell the children that on the count of three they will stand while still holding the parachute. Count to three and then stand.

4. Sing "The Wheels on the Bus Go 'Round and 'Round." While you sing the first verse of the song, move around in a circle. Sit for the next verse, and sing, "The bell on the bus goes ding, ding, ding."

5. For the next verse, grip the parachute firmly, stand, and wave it from side to side as you sing, "The wipers on the bus go swish, swish, swish."

6. Still holding the parachute, lie down so all the children's legs are under the parachute, as if they were fast asleep, and sing, "The babies on the bus go zzz, zzz, zzz."

7. Stand and wave the parachute up and down, with the children jumping up and down. As the children jump, sing "The children on the bus jump up and down."

8. Teach the children how to "mushroom" the parachute. Tell the children to stand and hold the chute at waist height. When everyone is set, tell them that on the count of three they will lift their arms over their heads to waft the chute high in the air and, as it billows, take one step forward, bring the parachute down behind them, and sit on the edge of the material. This will take practice, but the children will love to try it!

Another Idea …

● "Here We Go 'Round the Mulberry Bush" also works well with practicing parachute skills. Sit on the floor, and during the chorus, instead of moving with the parachute, pass it around from hand to hand. Use actions that the children can do while they are seated, such as rocking side to side, touching toes, bouncing on bottoms, and so on.

Rocket Man!

Jet off into space with this number rhyme and game. It helps children learn how to count backward and to understand the concepts of *one more* and *one less*.

What You Need

▶ just a parachute

Vocabulary

- count down
- dizzy
- floating
- journey
- moon
- planets
- space
- spinning
- stars
- taut

What Children Learn

● To use number names accurately in play

● To use mathematical language to solve problems

● To enjoy and respond to rhymes and songs

What to Do

1. Try a parachute rocket launch.

2. Have the children hold the parachute taut at waist height.

3. Count down with the children from 10 to 0, and blast off. On "zero," waft the parachute high in the air, let go, and shout, "Blast off!" Everyone should stand back to avoid the parachute as it falls!

Other Ideas ...

● Make some stars and planets with paper, scissors, paint, and collage materials. Attach these to the inside of the parachute using ribbon or double-sided tape. Waft the chute gently up and down as you sing, "Twinkle, Twinkle, Little Star."

● "Mushroom" the decorated parachute. Tell the children to stand and hold the chute at waist height. When everyone is set, tell them that on the count of three they will lift their arms over their heads to waft the chute high in the air and, as it billows, take one step forward, bring the parachute down behind them, and sit quickly on the edge of the material. This may take some practice! Read *Whatever Next* by Jill Murphy, *Roaring Rockets* by Tony Mitton, or *I Want to Be an Astronaut* by Byron Barton.

In My Tent

Pretend the parachute is a tent and have a campout!

What You Need

▶ just a parachute

Vocabulary

- air
- along
- backward
- careful
- collapse
- escape
- mushroom
- pat
- shake
- stamp
- tent
- under

What Children Learn

- To experiment with different ways of moving
- To try new combinations of movements and gestures
- To move with control and coordination
- To be confident about trying new activities and ideas

What to Do

1. Spread the parachute flat on the floor and ask the children to stand around the edge.

2. "Mushroom" the parachute. Tell the children to stand and hold the chute at waist height. When everyone is set, tell them that on the count of three they will lift their arms over their heads to waft the chute high in the air and, as it billows, take one step forward, bring the parachute down behind them, and sit quickly on the edge of the material. This may take some practice! The parachute will form an air-filled dome or mushroom-like tent. Tell the children to stay seated. If they stand up the air will escape, and the tent will collapse!

3. While seated, sing an action song to the tune of "Here We Go 'Round the Mulberry Bush," doing all the actions. Some suggestions include "This is the way we pat the tent," "....stamp our feet," "....wave our hands," and "....shake our heads."

Tips: Because it will get hot under the parachute, it is best to keep the game short. Finish by having the children move out from under the "mushroom" tent so they are again standing and holding the edges of the parachute. Have the children gently waft the parachute up and down and then rest and relax to some quiet music at the end. Some children (and adults) may feel uncomfortable in a confined space. Be ready to collapse the parachute and start again or vary the game to meet the needs of everyone.

Other Ideas ...

- While inside the "mushroom," ask the children to wriggle around so that they are facing the edge of the tent and then roll backward so that their legs are up the side of the tent. Start with a gentle patting of feet on the side of the tent, gradually patting faster and faster, until the children are patting their feet as fast and high as they can go.

- Make a tent and pass a ball from child to child as quickly as possible. Add music to the game, passing the ball from child to child and stopping when the music stops.

- Make a tent again and pat balloons back and forth. See how far the children can stretch to retrieve the balloons without letting the tent collapse.

- Pass an action (wriggle your nose, clap, wave) around the circle.

Pond Life

This parachute game uses familiar action songs and rhymes. Give your old favorites a new twist. Many well-known rhymes are suitable for parachute play.

What You Need

▶ just a parachute

Vocabulary

- calm
- choppy
- fast
- into
- jump
- pond
- ripples
- slow
- under
- waves

What Children Learn

- To sing and dance
- To begin to move rhythmically
- To listen with enjoyment and respond to stories, songs, rhymes, and poems

What to Do

1. Spread the parachute flat on the floor and ask the children to sit around the edge of the parachute "pond."

2. Choose 10 children to be frogs. (If there are fewer than 10 children in your group, change the lyrics to match the number of children.)

3. Have the children hold the parachute just a few inches above the ground and waft it gently to make small ripples in the pond.

4. Sing "Ten Little Speckled Frogs" (available on many CDs), with each frog jumping into the pond (over the small ripples that the children holding the parachute are creating).

5. Each time you finish a verse, one child jumps out of the parachute pond and joins the group wafting the parachute. You can play this game with any number of frogs.

Tip: If there are many young children in your group, it may be best to start with three "frogs."

Other Ideas ...

● Add some paper fishes to the pond. Say the poem "1, 2, 3, 4, 5, Once I Caught a Fish Alive!"

● Choose five children to be little ducks waddling around the pond and sing and perform the actions of "Five Little Ducks Went Swimming One Day."

● Make different kinds of waves on the pond. Ask, *Can you make a quiet and still pond?* Make the waves bigger and bigger, then smaller and smaller. Ask, *Can you make huge slow waves, and fast smaller ripples?*

Can You Guess How Many?

Math concepts take on new and real-life meaning when children use their bodies to solve math problems.

Vocabulary

- check
- estimate
- fewer
- fold
- greater
- half
- head-to-toe
- less than
- quarter
- test

What Children Learn

● To use mathematical language to solve problems

● To interact with others and work together toward a common goal

● To be confident about trying new activities

What to Do

1. Estimate with the children how many children would fit across the parachute if they were lined up head to toe. Write down the different estimates that the children give.

2. Lay the parachute flat on the floor. Invite some children to lie on the parachute in head-to-toe fashion. When they reach from one edge to the other, ask the other children to count how many children are lying down.

3. Next, ask them to estimate how many children would fit if the parachute was folded in half or quarters? Write down the estimates and then check them. Were their estimates greater than or less than the actual number? Do the children see any pattern in the number of children needed when the parachute is folded in half or in quarters? (For

example, when the parachute is folded in half, the number of children needed to reach from the fold to the edge is approximately half the number of children needed for the full parachute.)

4. Engage the children in a discussion about estimating.

Another Idea ...

● Lay the parachute flat on the floor, and ask one child to lie on a segment with her feet pointing toward the center and her arms spread wide. Invite another child to lie next to her so their outstretched arms touch. Keep adding on until the circle is complete. Ask, *How many children are needed to complete the parachute circle?*

Under the Big Top!

Use a colorful parachute to play this game about a circus.

What You Need

▶ just a parachute

Vocabulary

- acrobat
- big top
- chant
- circle
- circus

- clown
- edge
- laugh
- lion tamer
- play

- question
- respond
- rhyme
- tightrope
- tightrope walker

What Children Learn

- To move with confidence
- To work as part of a group
- To express and communicate their ideas by using a widening range of imagination and role-play and movement
- About the circus

What to Do

1. Spread the parachute flat on the floor.

2. Help the children stand evenly spaced around the edge of the parachute.

3. Ask all the children to sit, and then ask them what they know about the circus. Listen to their responses and continue to ask open-ended questions about the circus.

4. Teach them the following rhyme:

   Big Top Day by Jennifer Galvin

   It's going to be a big top day.
   We'll have some fun and play away.
   And when the circus comes today,
   We'll learn and read and laugh and play.

5. Once the children know the rhyme, ask them to stand and say it again while walking around in a circle and holding the parachute.

6. After the children recite it a few times, ask them to walk toward the center of the room while wafting the parachute up high to create a "big top." If you like, you can have them "mushroom" the parachute, so they can remain under the "big top." (See directions to "mushroom" the parachute on page 15.) Invite the children to come into the center of the circle and pretend to be acrobats, lion tamers, tightrope walkers, clowns, and so on.

Another Idea ...

- Play Popcorn and Cotton Candy with the children. Have the children hold the parachute at waist height. Go around the circle and alternate naming each child "popcorn" or "cotton candy." When everyone is ready, tell the children to waft the parachute up. Call out, *Popcorn!* and encourage all the children who are "popcorn" to run to the middle of the chute and jump around like kernels of popcorn. Then say, *Stop!* The "popcorn" children return to the edge of the parachute. Repeat the game, calling out, *Cotton candy!* These children run to the middle and pretend to be sticky cotton candy—once they touch someone else they become attached.

The Parachute Pokey

What You Need
▶ just a parachute

Try another version of the Hokey Pokey!

Vocabulary

- cross
- flight
- left/right
- open/shut
- sing
- softly/loudly
- stand up/kneel down
- straight
- up/around
- up/down

shake it all around!

What Children Learn

● To listen and respond to what they hear
● To share their ideas with others
● To interact with others and work together toward a common goal

What to Do

1. Have the children hold the parachute at waist height.

2. Then tell them they must work together as they move the parachute to the words of this song, which follows the tune of "The Hokey Pokey":

You move the parachute up,

You move the parachute down.

You move the parachute up,

And you shake it all around.

You shake it to the left,

You shake it to the right,

It's called the parachute flight.

3. Add variety by trying some of the following ideas while the children are holding the parachute, singing the song, and doing the actions. Suggestions include:
   - Keep your arms straight.
   - Cross your arms.
   - Hold the parachute with one hand (or two hands).
   - Move the parachute while standing up (or kneeling down).
   - Sing with your eyes open (or shut).
   - Sing softly (or loudly).
   - Just the boys (or the girls) sing.

4. Encourage the children to suggest their own ideas and then try their ideas.

Another Idea ...
- Add scarves, feathers, foam blocks, balloons, and other objects to the tossing fun.

   Note: Don't over inflate the balloons—it makes them harder to grasp and catch. Collect any burst balloons immediately. They present a potential choking hazard.

Dinosaur Parachute Play

What You Need
- just a parachute

Children love dinosaurs and this game gets them up and moving and pretending to be those prehistoric creatures.

Vocabulary

- back/forth
- apatosaurus
- dinosaur
- fast/slowly
- flap
- footstep
- imagination
- imitate
- move
- practice
- pretend
- pterodactyl
- stegosaurus
- swish
- tyrannosaurus rex
- up/down
- work together

What Children Learn

- To move in different ways
- To learn about dinosaurs and how they move
- To interact with others and work together toward a common goal

Apatosaurus!

What to Do

1. Spread the parachute flat on the floor and stand around it. Ask the children to lift it up to waist height.

2. Practice moving the parachute up and down so the children learn how to work together.

3. Move the parachute to imitate the movement of different dinosaurs. Following are some examples:

    - Pterodactyl: Raise the parachute up and down like a pterodactyl flapping its wings.

    - Apatosaurus: Raise the parachute as high as possible because this dinosaur was so tall.

    - Stegosaurus: Wave the parachute rapidly back and forth like the stegosaurus's tail, which it swished back and forth at its enemies.

    - Tyrannosaurus rex: Raise the parachute up slowly, then pull it down slowly, resembling a dinosaur taking big footsteps.

4. Encourage the children to suggest their own ideas for imitating the movement of different dinosaurs and then try their ideas.

Another Idea ...

- Do a Dino Dance with the children. Waft the parachute into the air, and call out the names of five or six children. Be sure to keep enough children holding onto the chute. The children whose names are called run under the parachute and do a Dino Dance, pretending to dance like the dinosaur of their choice. Encourage the other children to try to guess the type of dinosaur the children have chosen by the way they dance.

Playing Parachute Games with Props

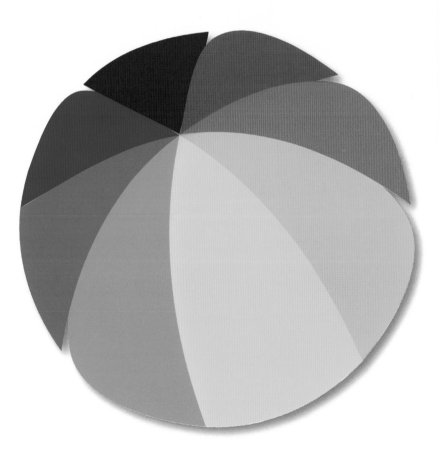

Criss Cross

A game for rolling, creeping, crawling, and changing places under a rolled parachute

What You Need

▸ parachute
▸ 3 different sound makers (for example, bells, shakers, and wooden blocks)

Vocabulary

- backward
- crawl
- creep
- fly
- forward
- hop
- reach
- space
- stretch
- swim
- travel
- under

What Children Learn

- To move in a variety of ways with control and coordination
- To move with confidence and imagination and in safety
- To experiment with different ways of moving
- To listen and then respond with comments, questions, and actions

What to Do

1. Play the different sound makers as the children listen to them. Talk about the different sounds.

2. Choose a movement for each sound. For example, rolling over when they hear the bells, crab walking to the drum, crawling on tummies to the wooden blocks, and so on. When a sound stops, the children must stop moving.

3. Try this out, helping any children who need it.

4. Now lay the parachute flat on the floor. With the children's help, fold it in half, and then roll it into a long sausage shape.

5. Help each child find a partner, or form groups of three. Two adults hold the rolled-up parachute about 20" above the floor.

6. A third adult plays an instrument to signal the actions for the first pair or group of children. The children roll, creep, or crawl under the chute as the instrument plays.

7. Allow each group to travel under the rolled-up parachute.

Other Ideas ...

- Change the sound and action several times as the children travel under the chute, so they change from crawling to creeping, and so on.
- Try the game with bunny hopping, slithering, and crawling, using hands and feet but no knees on the floor!
- Play the game with the children traveling backward.
- Call out different animal names. The first group slithers along under the rolled-up parachute as a snake, the next swims along like a fish, and so on.

Ten in the Bed

Children learn counting skills and the concept of *one less* while having tons of fun!

What You Need
- parachute
- ten children
- shaker, tambourine, or noisemaker

Vocabulary

- circle
- colors
- count
- curve
- edge
- half
- less
- more
- remaining
- roll over
- semicircle
- shapes
- slide
- straight

What Children Learn

- To say and use numbers in order
- To find *one more* and *one less* than a number from one to ten

What to Do

1. Spread the parachute flat on the floor, and with the children's help, fold the parachute carefully in half to make a semicircle shape. Talk about the different shapes and colors they can see. Ask, *What other semicircles can you find in the room?*

2. Ask the children to slide under the straight edge of the parachute, lying flat on their backs next to each other, with just their heads sticking out, as if they were all in a bed together.

3. Sing the "Ten in the Bed" song. When you sing "roll over, roll over," help the child closest to one end to roll over and out from under the parachute. Help the children count how many are left in the bed.

4. Give the first child out a shaker, tambourine, or noisemaker.

5. Sing the next verse: "There were nine in the bed…." At "roll over," the first child shakes the shaker and helps the next child to roll out.

6. Count the remaining children under the parachute, and let the next child take a turn with the shaker.

7. Before the next verse, ask the children how many will be left when another child rolls over and out from under the parachute. Talk about the concept of *one less*, or perhaps even *two less*.

Other Ideas …

● Play this game with lots of teddy bears. Guess how many teddy bears are in bed? Estimate and then count to check.

● Change the verses to "There were children in the bed, and the little one said, 'sit up'…,''roll onto your tummies…,''curl up small…,''stretch your arms in the air…,' 'show me ten fingers …,'" and so on.

Rainbow Fun

Use a parachute and some balloons to play this game that explores colors and patterns.

What You Need

- parachute
- lots of balloons (all colors)
- balloon pump

Vocabulary

- color
- different
- edge
- first
- matching
- pattern
- same
- second
- sequence
- third
- throw
- tight

What Children Learn

- To find similarities and differences
- To notice patterns

What to Do

1. Use a pump to inflate some balloons.

2. Spread the parachute flat on the floor. Ask the children to sit around the parachute and hold its edges. Then have the children pull the parachute tight and lift it just a few inches off the floor.

3. As you throw the balloons onto the parachute, ask the children to call out the color of the balloons you are throwing. For example, throw red, then blue, then red again, then blue again, and so on. Stop and ask the children which color balloon should come next.

4. Let the children move the parachute up and down until all the balloons have bounced off the parachute.

5. Play again, extending the activity by using a sequence of three different colors of balloons.

   Note: Don't over inflate the balloons—it makes them harder to grasp and catch.

   Safety note: Collect any burst balloons immediately. They are a potential choking hazard.

Other Ideas ...

● Spread the parachute flat on the floor. Ask the children to match the balloons to each colored section of the parachute.

● Lift the parachute and then throw lots of different balloons under it. One child or adult throws a color die or spins a color spinner. The children take turns crawling under the parachute to find a balloon that matches the color on the die or spinner.

Note: You may want to lift the parachute a bit off the floor to make it easier for the children to find the right color balloon.

● Put different colored stickers on the balloons, such as a red balloon with a green sticker. Roll the balloons onto the top of the parachute. Shake the parachute gently so that one balloon falls off. Ask one child to retrieve the balloon and name the color of the balloon and the color of the sticker.

Skip This Way, Skip That Way

What You Need

▶ name card for each child

▶ parachute

Use this game to help children practice skipping techniques, taking turns, and learning to work together.

Vocabulary

- fast
- grip
- high
- left
- letter
- low
- names
- pair
- partner
- recognize
- right
- skip
- slow
- slowly

What Children Learn

● To learn how to work together with adults and peers

● To get along with a group

● To begin to recognize names and other words

● To enjoy dancing and singing games

What to Do

1. Shuffle the name cards and put them face down in a pile on the floor away from the parachute.

2. Spread the parachute flat on the floor. Ask the children to sit around the edge of the parachute, grip the edge, and slowly stand.

3. Wave the parachute up and down together.

4. Invite one child to skip around the edge of the parachute and over to the pile of name cards. This child takes the top card and reads the name on the card. If the child cannot read yet, help him recognize the first letter of the name and tell him the name.

5. While the group holds the parachute up high, the child skips under the parachute to the child whose name is on the card.

6. Those two children skip around under the parachute as the others hold the parachute high in the air and sing a song, such as "Here We Go Looby Loo," "Here We Go 'Round the Mulberry Bush," or any other song.

7. Encourage the children who are skipping to hold hands and skip together. When the song finishes, the child closest to skipping pair is the next to choose a name card and then a partner.

Other Ideas …

● Have the children hold onto the parachute at about waist height as they walk around in a circle, and then put their left legs, their right legs, and other parts of their bodies into the circle to the tune and words of the "Hokey Pokey."

● Play some music and encourage the children to waft the parachute up and down. When the music stops, turn over two name cards. Call out (or help the children call out) the names. The two children whose names are called run under or around the parachute to swap places before the music starts again.

Matching Pairs

Use a parachute to explore different ways of matching and sorting pictures and objects.

What You Need

▶ parachute

▶ matching pairs of objects (socks, keys, hats, and other everyday objects)

Vocabulary

- another
- describe
- different
- like
- many
- match
- nearly
- objects
- pair
- same
- single
- sort

What Children Learn

- To ask simple questions
- To exchange ideas
- To extend their vocabulary, exploring the meaning and sound of new words
- To use talking to clarify their thinking
- To look closely at similarities and differences

What to Do

1. Place the pairs of objects on the floor and spread the parachute over the objects. Sit around the edge of the parachute with the children.

2. Let the children take turns diving under the parachute to find an object. When everyone has had a turn, talk about the different objects, and then challenge the children to find the objects that match.

3. Put all the objects back under the parachute.

4. Ask one child to dive under the parachute and find a particular object. Name the object you want the child to find or describe the object by its use, such as, "Find something that opens doors."

5. Ask the next child to dive under and find the matching object (in this instance, it would be the other key). Make it more exciting by counting to ten (slowly) with the other children to see if the diver can find the object before the children reach ten!

Other Ideas ...

● Ask all the children to remove one shoe and place it under the parachute. Hold the parachute at the children's waist height and walk around in a circle. Call the names of three or four children, who then dive under the parachute to find and put on their lost shoe!

● Put pairs of socks, gloves, and dress-up shoes under the parachute. Have the children take turns diving under the parachute to choose a pair of items and put them on, until all the children are wearing pairs of clothing.

Color Swap

A parachute game for finding, using, and recognizing colors

What You Need

- small blocks (two of each color) enough for one per child
- parachute

Vocabulary

- change
- colors
- listen
- next to
- part
- remember
- segment
- shape
- swap
- turn
- under

What Children Learn

- To listen and respond to what they hear
- To try new activities
- To work as part of a group
- To be aware of space, themselves, and others

What to Do

1. Spread the parachute flat on the floor.

2. Ask the children to stand around the edge of the parachute.

3. Ask each child in turn to call out the color of the segment of the parachute she is standing next to.

4. Call out one of the parachute colors and the name of a child standing next to that color. This child then runs round the edge of the parachute to the next segment of the same color.

5. She gently touches the child already standing by this segment on the shoulder and takes her place. This child then moves to the next segment of the same color, touches that child, takes her place, and so on.

6. Play this game for each color on the parachute, so all the children have a turn.

Other Ideas ...

- Vary the game by changing the colors and where the children are standing.

- Hold the parachute very close to the floor, so the children swapping places need to slither across under the chute.

- Play the game with different color shapes, such as red circles or blue squares. The children with the same color shapes trade places.

Popcorn

Work together (and have lots of fun!) bouncing balloons and balls on, off, under, and over a parachute.

What You Need

- beach balls, balloons, or rolled-up pairs of socks (or a mixture of these)
- parachute

Vocabulary

- balloon
- big/small
- bounce
- fast
- first/last
- heavy
- high/low
- light
- on/off
- predict
- shudder
- slow
- under/over
- waft

What Children Learn

- To work as part of a group, taking turns and sharing fairly
- To use words to organize, sequence, and clarify their thinking
- To ask questions about why things happen and how things work

What to Do

1. Spread the parachute flat on the floor.
2. Ask the children to stand around the edge and lift the parachute up to their waist height.
3. Start by throwing one balloon into the middle of the parachute. Waft the parachute up and down together, and see how quickly you can work to bounce the balloon off the parachute.
4. Throw lots of balloons onto the parachute and play again.
5. Experiment with big and small movements, wafting the parachute high and low, or making little shakes and shudders. Ask the children to predict what might happen to the balloons with each movement.
6. Try this again with beach balls. How high will they bounce? What about rolled-up pairs of socks? Are they heavier or lighter, larger or smaller?

7. Put all the items on the parachute. Which will bounce off first? Which will be last to fall?

Note: Don't over inflate the balloons—it makes them harder to grasp and catch. Collect any burst balloons immediately. They are a potential choking hazard.

Other Ideas ...

- Use a marker to write each child's name on a balloon. Throw all the balloons onto the parachute. Shake it and see which name comes off first. Which one is last to bounce off the chute?

- Write each child's name on a strip of paper and bounce these like popcorn on the parachute. Each child can throw his or her name back onto the parachute as it is bounced off.

Into the Bucket You Go!

What You Need
- small blanket (not a parachute)
- bucket
- teddy bears and other soft toys
- small balls (sponge/plastic)
- parachute

Use this game to let children practice working together to make something happen. This game is more difficult than it looks!

Vocabulary

- backward
- blanket
- bucket
- catch
- forward
- gentle
- high
- hold
- low
- roll
- sideways
- slide
- steep
- taut
- tip

What Children Learn

- To go backward and sideways as well as forward
- To move with control and coordination
- To be aware of space, others, and themselves

What to Do

1. Choose two children to hold a blanket and two more to hold a bucket. They need to stand near the parachute, one pair on each side of it.

2. Ask the rest of the children to hold the parachute tightly at waist height and step backward so that the parachute is held taut and as flat as possible.

3. Put some balls on the parachute and work together with the children to tip the parachute gently so that the balls roll toward the edge for the other children to catch on the blanket or in the bucket. You probably need to say which!

4. Stop and talk about what happened and how the children need to move to be more successful.

5. Try again and see if the children's technique improves.

6. Put some teddy bears or soft toys on the parachute. Can the children tip or roll them onto the blanket or into the bucket?

7. Talk again about which way the parachute needs to be tipped. Try fast and slow movements and high and low movements.

Other Ideas ...

- Put three soft toys on the taut parachute and bounce them up and down as the children sing "Three Little Monkeys Jumping on the Bed."

- Put a doll on the parachute and rock the doll while the children sing "Rock-a-bye Baby" or other lullabies.

Set the Sails, Land Ahoy!

What You Need
- parachute
- treasure chest or box
- pirate or sailor clothes, hats, earrings, "telescopes," and any other pirate- or sailor-related accessory
- 2 adults

Use a parachute to make a boat for a group of children. Make some sailor or pirate props, climb aboard, and sail away, singing your favorite sea songs and shanties.

Vocabulary
- backward
- forward
- move
- ocean
- pretend
- rock
- sea
- sideways
- slowly/fast
- song
- telescope
- treasure
- waves

What Children Learn
- To move rhythmically
- To learn songs and match movements to music
- To express and communicate their ideas
- To be aware of space, others, and themselves
- To move with control and coordination

What to Do
1. Make some props—telescopes from cardboard tubes, scarves for head-dresses, and any other sailor- or pirate-related props.
2. Write the names of all the sea songs and poems you know on bits of paper and put them into the treasure chest. Examples include
   - "Anchors Aweigh,"
   - "I Saw a Ship A-Sailing,"
   - "Michael, Row Your Boat Ashore,"
   - "Row, Row, Row Your Boat,"
   - "Sailing, Sailing,"
   - "A Sailor Went to Sea, Sea, Sea."

3. Invite the children to dress in sailor or pirate outfits.

4. Lay the parachute flat on the floor. With another adult's help, roll and fold the sides of the parachute in to make an approximate rectangle shape.

5. Sit with the children on the parachute, in a line, one behind the other, all facing the same way. Have the children lift the sides to form the edge of the boat.

6. Ask one of the children to choose a slip of paper from the treasure chest. Sing the song, rocking the boat forward and backward together.

7. Try another song, rocking gently from side to side.

8. Try singing with one child standing to look through a telescope as the boat moves from side to side in a storm!

Other Ideas ...

● Cut an anchor shape from cardboard and attach it to the parachute with ribbon. Pull the anchor onto your boat, working together to heave the anchor out of the water.

● Read a book about the sea as you gently rock from side to side.

● Have the children make their own telescopes (decorated cardboard tubes, with cellophane lenses) and climb aboard the parachute ship. Help each child describe, but not name, what he can see through his telescope. Can the other children guess what they are looking at? You may need to help younger children by modeling this yourself.

● First describe and then make the sounds of the sea, using a rainstick, shakers, drums, or other musical instruments. Ask, *Is it calm water or a choppy sea; are there rolling waves or a raging storm?* Move the parachute together to match the sounds you make.

Traffic Lights

Parachute play can help children learn and understand games with rules and develop listening skills. Use this game for learning and fun!

What You Need

▶ 3 sound makers (for example, wooden blocks, a shaker, bells, or a castanet)

▶ parachute

Vocabulary

- different
- fast/slow
- high
- kick
- listen
- low
- next
- pace
- shake
- stop/go
- together

What Children Learn

● To listen and then respond to what they have heard

● To be confident about trying new activities and ideas

● To move with confidence and imagination

● To move with control and coordination

● To experiment with different ways of moving

What to Do

1. Spread the parachute flat on the floor and sit with the children around its edge with everyone's legs under the chute.

2. Explain to the children that this is a listening game.
   - When the children hear the wooden blocks, they should lift the parachute as high as they can, while still staying seated.
   - When the children hear the shaker, they should shake the parachute vigorously at floor level.
   - When the children hear the bells or castanet, they should lie back, still holding the parachute, and kick their legs up and down under the chute.

3. Start the game slowly, but gradually quicken the pace.

4. When the children are confident with this game, challenge them to try it with their eyes closed!

Another Idea ...
- Play again with different instruments and bigger movements, such as standing and sitting while holding the parachute, letting go and swiveling around when seated and then grabbing the edge of the parachute again, or lying flat on their tummies with their arms stretched out in front of them. Ask the children to suggest new actions.

Follow My Lead

Adding a parachute to this game makes it harder but more fun to do! It also gives children practice in imitating actions and taking turns.

What You Need

- parachute
- small stickers (2 colors)
- soft balls (sponge or fabric)

Vocabulary

- backward
- catch
- color
- copy
- crawl
- follow
- forward
- hop
- imitate
- kick
- leader
- like
- look
- pat
- push
- same
- shuffle
- similar
- sticker
- take turns
- throw
- touch
- watch
- weave

What Children Learn

- To be aware of space, others, and themselves
- To control an object by touching, pushing, patting, throwing, catching, and kicking it
- To interact with others, negotiating activities and taking turns in conversations

What to Do

1. Spread the parachute flat on the floor and sit around the edge with the children.

2. Give each child a sticker, alternating the two colors. Ask them to put their stickers on their shirts where they can see them. Ask them to tell you what color sticker they have. Be sure all of the children know which color they are wearing.

3. Stand up together, holding the parachute at about waist height. Throw the balls under the parachute.

4. Ask all the children with a sticker of one color to let go of the parachute, find a ball, and then come back to their places.

5. Now ask one child to be the leader, and weave in and out of the children who are holding the parachute, ducking under the parachute as necessary. The other children with the same color sticker follow the leader.

6. Play again, calling out the other color so that everyone has a chance to play.

7. Try lots of different actions, perhaps hopping along, crawling, shuffling on bottoms, and so on, both forward and backward.

Other Ideas ...

- Play again, with the leader changing her actions several times on the way around the circle.

- Play Follow My Lead with balloons, with the leader traveling over and under the parachute with a balloon, perhaps tapping it from hand to hand, perhaps holding it between her elbows, perhaps with it behind her back.

  Note: Do not over inflate the balloons—it makes them harder to grasp and catch. Collect any burst balloons immediately. They are a potential choking hazard.

Animals Everywhere

Add some simple props to a parachute game to make it lively and creative!

Vocabulary

- crawl
- creep
- hop
- imagination
- imitate
- plod
- prowl
- scurry
- slither
- trade
- trample

What Children Learn

- To sing and move their bodies in different ways
- To interact with others, taking turns in conversations
- To develop their vocabulary, exploring the meaning and sound of new words

What to Do

1. Make enough cardboard animal shapes so that each child has one. Give each child a cardboard animal shape.

2. The children place their animal shapes on the floor beside their feet or behind them.

3. Have the children hold the parachute at waist height and wave it up and down.

4. Call out one of the animal names, and help the children with that animal shape travel under the parachute, moving like that animal to change places with another child who has the same cardboard animal shape.

Another Idea ....

● "Mushroom" the parachute. Tell the children to stand and hold the chute at their waist height. When everyone is set, tell them that on the count of three they will lift their arms over their heads to waft the chute high in the air and, as it billows, take one step forward, bring the parachute down behind them, and quickly sit on the edge of the material. This may take some practice. Sing "One Elephant Went Out to Play, Upon a Spider's Web One Day" while in the "mushroom," or sing the following song to the tune of "Here We Go 'Round the Mulberry Bush":

We went to visit the zoo one day.

We saw some elephants across the way.

What do you think we saw them do?

Swing, swing, swing their trunks.

Swing your arm in front of you like an elephant's trunk. Repeat with other animals.

Names, Names, Names!

What You Need

▶ parachute

▶ shoulder bag

▶ name card for each child

A great way to practice first-letter sounds, letters, and names!

Vocabulary

- circle
- direction
- find
- letter
- listen
- name
- pass
- recognize
- sound
- turn
- waist
- word

What Children Learn

● To hear and say sounds in words in the order in which they occur

● To read familiar and common words

● To form good relationships with adults and peers

What to Do

1. Put the children's name cards in a pile.

2. Turn these over one by one, and as each child recognizes his own name, let him put it into the bag. Talk about the first letters and first-letter sounds on each name card.

3. Spread the parachute flat on the floor and stand around the edge with the children. Have them lift the parachute to waist height.

4. Sing "A Tisket, A Tasket" as they move around in a circle with the parachute.

5. Stop the music.

6. Pull two name cards from the bag, and ask these children to run under the parachute to change places.

7. Play again. Continue until the bag is empty and all the children have had a turn. Each time you sing the song, change the direction the circle moves (once to the right, then to the left, back to the right, and so on).

A Tisket, A Tasket

A tisket, a tasket,
A green and yellow basket.
I wrote a letter to my love,
And on the way I dropped it.

I dropped it, I dropped it,
And on the way I dropped it.
A little boy (girl) picked it up,
And put it in his (her) pocket.

Other Ideas ...

- Place all the name cards face up on the floor under the parachute. Have the children sit down and hold the parachute about 8" above the floor. Invite children in groups of three to dive under the parachute and find their names.

- Waft the parachute up and down, and then call out, *If your name begins with an* S, *dive under.* Let the parachute fall gently onto the heads of the children who have dived under the parachute. Bring it up slowly and check that you have caught the right children underneath it!

All Dressed Up

Use your parachute to help children practice dressing skills and how to help each other. Add some unusual things such as flippers, arm bands, rubber boots, fluffy slippers, long socks, raincoats, hats, wigs, and any other dress-up clothes.

What You Need

- parachute
- dress-up clothes with easy fastenings
- sand or other kind of timer

Vocabulary

- body parts
- bottom
- fastener words
- help
- next
- sleeve
- together
- top

What Children Learn

- To dress and undress independently
- To interact with others
- To consider the consequences of their words and actions
- To speak clearly with confidence and control and to be aware of the listener

What to Do

1. Spread the parachute flat on the floor.

2. Ask everyone to choose a dress-up item, bring it to the parachute, and sit around the edge.

3. Ask the child next to you to stand. Start the timer and ask that child to put on her dress-up item, with the help of the child next to her.

   Note: Change the amount of time on the timer to reflect the ages and skills of the children in the group. The children should feel challenged but able to finish in time so they also feel successful.

4. As soon as the first child is finished, the next child puts on her dress-up item with the help of the next child, and so on.

5. Continue around the parachute. Can the children make it completely around the chute before the timer is finished?

6. Next, lift the parachute together and waft it up and down.

7. When it is high in the air, call out an item of clothing, such as "hat." All the children with hats let go of the parachute and cross under the parachute before the chute falls to the floor.

Another Idea ...

- Put hats and shoes under the parachute. Ask all the children wearing blue to find a hat, then all the children wearing yellow to find a shoe. Continue with other colors.

First-Letter Sounds

What You Need

- parachute
- shoebox with a lid
- small objects, such as an apple, ball, car, toy dog, and block

Explore everyday objects and listen for first-letter sounds with this parachute game. You need some small objects that begin with clear, single sounds.

Vocabulary

- box
- collapse
- color
- high
- inside
- letter
- like
- mushroom
- object
- same
- similar
- sound
- start
- tent
- waft

What Children Learn

- To develop vocabulary, exploring the meaning and sound of new words
- To link sounds to letters, naming and sounding the letters of the alphabet
- To hear and say letter sounds in words in the order in which they appear

What to Do

1. Show the children the objects you will use and help them say the first letter sound of each one.

2. "Mushroom" the parachute. Tell the children to stand and hold the chute at waist height. When everyone is set, tell them that on the count of three they will lift their arms over their heads to waft the chute high in the air and, as it billows, take one step forward, bring the parachute down behind them, and quickly sit on the edge of the material. The air trapped inside the parachute creates a "mushroom" or tent. Remind the children to stay seated, or the air will escape and the parachute will collapse!

3. Place three or four objects in the box, put the lid on, and slide the box across the mushroom tent to a child.

4. Ask the child to look inside the box and tell everyone the first-letter sound of one of the objects it contains. Can the children guess what it might be? Give clues and prompts. Ask, *Is it something that you can eat?* Encourage the child to describe the object by its use, color, shape, and other attributes.

5. When one of the children guesses correctly, slide the box to that child and continue to play the game. Add more objects to the box as necessary.

Other Ideas …

● Give all the children a small picture of an object (perhaps from a lotto or pairs game). Ask them to call out the name of the object and the first-letter sound one at a time. Then have them pick up the parachute and pull it taut. Hold it with just one hand each and walk in one direction around the circle. Every so often, stop and call out a first-letter sound. Children with pictures of objects that begin with the same first-letter sound quickly cross under the parachute to the opposite side and continue to play the game.

● Give each child a sticky note with a letter on it. Use pairs of letters so that you can call out different letters and ask the children to swap places.

Up and Down, Side to Side

What You Need

- parachute
- simple instruments (shaker, tambourine, bells)
- drum music on a CD or tape

Get physical with this lively game of marching, kicking, hopping, and stamping! It also helps develop listening skills.

Vocabulary

- beat
- drum
- fast
- follow
- instrument
- listen
- march
- music
- next
- pace
- rhythm
- side
- slow
- taut
- up/down

What Children Learn

- To move with confidence and imagination
- To experiment with different ways of moving
- To work as part of a group
- To be concerned about others
- To consider the consequences of their words and actions for others and themselves

What to Do

1. Spread the parachute flat on the floor and sit with the children around it. Have everyone pick the parachute up by its edge and hold it taut.
2. Have everyone stretch their legs under the parachute, continuing to keep it taut.
3. Start the drum music, and kick to the rhythm under the parachute.
4. Next, have everyone stand and pull the parachute taut again. Let go of the parachute with one hand and stand sideways to it, everyone facing in the same direction.

5. March to the drum music, but ask the children to listen for the bell, shaker, or other instrument. When they hear this, they should swap hands, turn around, and change direction.

6. Try this several times with one instrument before adding another sound to the game. When the children hear the next sound, they should quickly sit and stand again, and when everyone is ready, continue marching in the same direction.

7. Quicken the pace for older children.

8. Emphasize the importance of not bumping into each other and working as part of a team.

Other Ideas ...

- Practice moving forward and backward, in and out of the circle with the parachute. Try crawling forward and backward, holding the parachute. Take giant strides, jump, or even hop like a bunny while holding the parachute!

- Hold the parachute and chant the following as you do the actions: "Up and down, up and down, side to side, side to side, here we go again. Up and down, up and down, side to side, this is where we stop!"

- Play musical bumps. When the music stops, all the children dive under the parachute, leaving the adults holding the parachute above the children's heads. Ask the children to sit in different positions—legs outstretched, kneeling, legs crossed.

I Am the Music Man!

What You Need

▶ parachute

▶ sound makers (blocks, keys, spoons, pans, balloons)

▶ simple instruments

Making music and changing sounds are the focus of this game that uses all sorts of sound makers, not just instruments.

Vocabulary

- bang
- beat
- clang
- color
- drum
- high/low
- hiss
- instrument
- loud/soft
- music
- rattle
- ring
- shake
- sound
- sound maker
- tap

What Children Learn

● To explore the different sounds of instruments

● To begin to learn songs

● To recognize and explore how sounds can be changed

● To continue to be interested, excited, and motivated to learn

● To be confident about trying new activities

What to Do

1. Spread the parachute flat on the floor and ask each child to sit on a different-colored section.

2. Place all the instruments and sound makers in the middle.

3. Chant, "I am the music man, I come from far away, and I can play. What can you play? I can play the …." (Ask one child to choose an instrument.)

4. Talk about the different sounds this instrument makes, such as the bang of the drum. Ask all the children on the blue sections to find something from the middle to make a drum-like sound (tapping on a balloon, banging blocks together).

5. Chant the verse again, and when it gets to the last line, ask each child to play in turn ("I can play the drum," "I can play the balloon," "I can play the blocks," and so on).

6. Continue to play the game until all the children have had a turn with the instruments and sound makers.

7. Next, the adults hold the parachute high. Ask the drummer to lead the children around and under the parachute, follow-the-leader style, as you all chant, "We are the music men, we come from far away, and we can play …."

Note: Don't over inflate the balloons—it makes them harder to grasp and catch. Collect any burst balloons immediately. They are a potential choking hazard.

Other Ideas …

● Have the children sit and hold the parachute taut just above ground level. Add tiny bells to the top of the parachute. Ask, *How can you change the sounds they make?*

● Have the children hold the parachute taut, just high enough for them to wriggle under. Hide some sound makers and instruments under the parachute. Invite a child to wriggle under, choose a sound maker, and slither to the other side without making a sound.

Count Down!

Use a parachute to help children learn counting and number recognition with these simple games.

What You Need
- parachute
- a large floor die with numbers or dots
- 21 plastic blocks or counters
- number cards 1–6

Vocabulary
- around
- block
- count
- dance
- die
- estimate
- guess
- less
- more
- number
- same
- together
- turn

What Children Learn
- To count up to six objects from a larger group
- To recognize some numerals
- To say and use number names in order
- To use words such as *more* or *less* to compare two numbers
- To work as part of a group, taking turns and sharing fairly

What to Do

1. Spread the parachute flat on the floor.

2. Stand at the edge with the children and lift the parachute to the children's waist height. Spread plastic blocks or counters under the parachute. Put the number cards on the floor outside the parachute circle.

3. The children take turns throwing the die on the floor outside the circle.

4. Count the number of spots together.

5. The thrower then dives under the parachute to collect that number of blocks or counters. As the child dives under the parachute, waft it up and down in huge movements, or dance around in a circle.

6. Ask the child to count the number of blocks he collected and place the blocks on the card with the correct numeral.

7. Continue to take turns throwing the die until all the cards have the right number of blocks. If a number is thrown that has already been completed, pass the die to the next child.

8. Play again until everyone has had a turn.

Other Ideas ...

● Have the children hold the parachute taut at waist height. Bounce a large soft foam die on top of the parachute. When it stops bouncing, count the number of spots, and that number of children let go of the parachute and sit in the middle underneath it. The remaining children will need to spread out to hold the parachute. Continue to play until the parachute finally collapses on the children in the middle!

● Throw a die and count the spots. Place that number of small soft toys on the parachute and bounce them gently up and down. Keep throwing the die and adding more soft toys. How many can be bounced without any falling off?

"The Itsy Bitsy Spider"

This game links to the popular topic of spiders, providing active, whole-body play (and learning) for children!

What You Need

- parachute
- spider puppet, soft toy, or homemade spider
- card in the shape of the sun

Vocabulary

- catch
- climb
- crawling
- creeping
- legs
- move
- moving
- pass around
- spider
- waist
- waterspout
- web
- wriggling

What Children Learn

- To ask questions about why things happen and how things work
- To investigate objects and materials by using their senses
- To listen with enjoyment and respond to stories, songs, music, rhymes, and poems

What to Do

1. Lay the parachute flat on the floor. Have the children sit at the edge of the parachute and gently pass the spider from one child to the next. When everyone has had a chance to hold the spider, ask one of the children to crawl onto the parachute with it. Talk about how a spider might move.

2. Now give small groups of three or four children a chance to move around on top of the parachute, trying out spider moves. Repeat until all children try it.

3. Invite another child to hold the sun shape and sing, "The Itsy Bitsy Spider." Do the actions together.

The Itsy Bitsy Spider

The itsy bitsy spider climbed up the waterspout.

Down came the rain and washed the spider out.

Out came the sun and dried up all the rain,

And the itsy bitsy spider climbed up the spout again!

4. Experiment with making rain sounds using the parachute—rubbing the material together or tapping it as the children hold it taut. If your parachute has a center hole and it is large enough, the child holding the sun shape can pop up through this hole.

5. Finish with a chasing parachute game. Hold the parachute at the adult's waist level, and ask one child to stand underneath the parachute with the spider. Tell the others they are a fly, a ladybug, or a bee (more than one child can be a fly, a ladybug, or a bee).

6. Call out one of the insects. These children need to cross under the parachute without being caught by the spider. If they are caught, let them rejoin the game for another turn.

7. Continue playing the game, letting the children take turns being the spider, until everyone has had a chance to try to escape the spider's clutches several times.

Other Ideas ...

- Read *The Very Hungry Caterpillar* by Eric Carle or *The Crunching Munching Caterpillar* by Sheridan Cain and Jack Tickle.

- Invite the children to take turns under the parachute to be wriggling caterpillars, squirming and writhing along.

- Give the children scarves or similar fabric so they can become butterflies emerging from their cocoons.

Up and Down Parachute Hill

What You Need
- parachute
- strong tape, scissors, chalk
- small cars, balls, cardboard tubes, beanbags

A game for investigating rolling by using a parachute for a different purpose.

Vocabulary
- bumpy
- distance
- estimate
- fast/slow
- hill
- light/heavy
- mark
- near/far
- release
- round
- smooth
- steep
- target
- up/down

What Children Learn
- To investigate objects and materials using their senses
- To look closely at similarities, differences, and patterns
- To ask questions about why things happen and how things work
- To use everyday words to describe where things are
- To use mathematical ideas and methods to solve practical problems

What to Do
1. Attach one edge of the parachute securely to a steady table, storage unit, or frame, at about table height. Secure the rest of the parachute to the floor with tape, pulling it taut to make a hill.
2. Use chalk or tape to make a target circle a distance away from the bottom of the parachute.
3. Ask every child to choose a car or other object to roll down the parachute hill. Ask them to choose something that they think may roll into the target area. Talk about the reasons for their choices. Ask open-ended questions and

encourage the children to think ahead, predict, and
develop their ideas.

4. Allow the children to take turns releasing the objects down
the parachute hill. Encourage them to mark where their
object landed, writing or copying their name from their
name cards with chalk or onto a piece of tape on the floor.

5. Try different objects, and help the children to work out why
some objects roll closer to the target than others.

Other Ideas ...

● Try varying the steepness of the hill. Ask the children for ideas on how to vary
the gradient. *What would happen if you put a box under the parachute hill to make
a hump on the track?*

● Ask the children to work in pairs rolling balls up and down the hill to each other.

● Use tape or ribbon to mark lanes on the hill. Roll the cars down the hill, counting
how many stay in their lane and how many cross over lanes. Use a clipboard to
record the results.

Target Time

Use a parachute to give children eye-hand coordination practice with these target games and activities.

What You Need

▶ parachute
▶ rolled-up pairs of socks
▶ small soft balls, rings
▶ beach balls or balloons

Vocabulary

- bounce
- catch
- edge
- fast/slow
- hands
- kick
- listen
- near/far
- partner
- pat
- push
- roll
- segment
- throw
- touch
- under/over

What Children Learn

● To control an object by touching, pushing, patting, throwing, catching, and kicking it

● To move with confidence and imagination

● To be aware of space, others, and themselves

What to Do

1. Spread the parachute flat on the floor and ask the children to sit near the center, one on each colored segment.

2. Sit a partner for each child at the outside edge of each colored segment.

3. The two children practice rolling the beach balls (or balloons) between them along each colored segment. Call out a color and ask the children on that segment to roll the ball to their partner. Call out different colors for different children, in quick succession.

4. The children try throwing the ball to each other. Call out different colors and then the word *roll* or *throw*. The children will need to listen for both parts of the instruction.

5. Try adding rings, rolled-up socks, and beach balls. The children can practice rolling, throwing, and catching these objects.

Note: Do not over inflate the balloons—it makes them harder to grasp and catch. Collect any burst balloons immediately. They are a potential choking hazard.

Other Ideas ...

- Play the same game, with the children kicking the beach balls to each other or patting balloons to each other.

- Have the children "mushroom" the parachute. Tell them to stand and hold the chute at child-waist height. When everyone is set, tell them that on the count of three they will lift their arms over their heads to waft the chute high in the air and, as it billows, take one step forward, bring the parachute down behind them, and sit on the edge of the material. The trapped air will create a "mushroom" or tent. They need to stay seated or the air will escape and the mushroom will collapse! Place a ring on a child's arm and ask her to pass it to the next child by sliding the ring down her arm and onto her neighbor's. Continue to pass the ring around the circle. Try passing rings from foot to foot, too!

- Spread the parachute flat on the floor and sort colored beanbags onto matching colored segments. Next, take turns trying to throw the beanbags into the hole or a basket placed at the center of the parachute.

"The Hokey Pokey"

What You Need
- parachute
- bell or chime

Play a new version of "The Hokey Pokey" in this singing game with plenty of action!

Vocabulary

- backward/ forward
- carefully
- in/out
- neighbor
- side to side
- space
- up/down

What Children Learn

- To go backward and sideways as well as forward
- To experiment with different ways of moving
- To be aware of space, others, and themselves
- To develop an awareness of their own needs, views, and feelings
- To be sensitive to the needs, views, and feelings of others

What to Do

1. Spread the parachute flat on the floor and sit around it with the children.

2. Tell the children that you are going to do "The Hokey Pokey" with the parachute. Ask them to help you figure out some rules that will make it safe for everyone, such as stopping if the person next to you falls, taking care not to bump into others, and so on.

3. Lift the parachute to the children's waist height and sing the song.

4. Encourage the children to use big, exaggerated movements.

5. Praise the children for adjusting their actions to fit their neighbor's.

6. Practice turning around, holding the chute with first one hand then the other as they turn.

7. Sound a bell or chime at frequent intervals to indicate that the children should change the direction of the circle. Encourage them to hold onto the parachute at all times.

Other Ideas ...

- Drape the parachute over some boxes to create a tunnel. Have the children scramble under the tunnel, forward, backward, sideways, on tummies, bottoms, hands and knees, or hands and feet.

- With the parachute at the children's waist height, play a crossover game in which children whose name begins with a particular first-letter sound swap places under the parachute, crossing over in a specified way, such as slithering backward, and crawling sideways. For jumping, hopping, skipping, and so on, raise the parachute to the appropriate height.

Jumping Rabbit!

Parachute games are great for practicing stretching and jumping.

What You Need

▶ parachute

▶ plenty of energy!

▶ 2 or 3 extra adults

Vocabulary

- bent/straight
- curled
- elephant
- frog
- giraffe
- high/low
- horse
- kangaroo
- practice
- rabbit
- small/tall
- spider
- stretch
- under
- underneath

What Children Learn

● To be aware of space, others, and themselves

● To move with control and coordination

● To move with confidence and imagination and in safety

● To express and communicate their ideas by using a widening range of imagination, role-play, and movement

What to Do

1. Lay the parachute flat on the floor. Sit around the edge of the chute and talk with the children about different animals that jump, such as kangaroos, rabbits, jumping spiders, frogs, and any other animals.

2. Try different ways that the animals might jump—on all fours, with two feet together, feet apart, legs straight, legs bent, and so on.

3. With other adults, hold the parachute high in the air and call out "jumping spider," "jumping kangaroo," "jumping rabbit," "jumping frog," and so on.

4. The children jump under the chute in the style of that animal. See if they can jump so their heads touch the underneath of the chute.

5. Next think of tall animals, such as elephants, horses, and giraffes. Talk about and try out the ways they can move. Have the children stretch their arms and legs to make big shapes and long tails. They should strut about under the parachute, reaching high and pretending to be one of the animals.

Other Ideas ...

- Stand, holding the chute high. Invite a child to cross under the parachute, chanting "My name is …, and I can jump high." He jumps across to another child, who then jumps back under the parachute to another child, perhaps doing bunny jumps, or tiny little jumps.

- Invite half the children to crouch really small on the floor. Hold the parachute with the other children, so it is resting gently on the backs of the crouched children. Chant "Small, small, small, getting taller, taller, taller, tall, tall, tall," gradually lifting the parachute as the children uncurl and stretch as tall as they can. Lower the parachute, slowly reversing, "Tall, tall, tall, getting smaller, smaller, smaller, small, small, small."

Forward, Backward, Sideways

Understanding directional words is an important literacy skill. What a fun way to learn these words!

Vocabulary

- backward/ forward
- bounce
- direction
- giant
- hide
- high/low
- middle
- sideways
- step
- tiny
- up/down

What Children Learn

- To move in a variety of ways with control and coordination
- To interact with others and work together toward a common goal
- To listen and respond to what they hear
- To be confident about trying new activities

What to Do

1. Have the children hold the parachute taut and try to move the whole chute forward, backward or sideways. Have them all move toward the middle so the parachute folds on the floor and then step slowly backward until it is taut. They should try this on tiptoes, with giant strides, or with tiny steps.

2. Put a soft teddy bear or other soft toy on the parachute. Bounce the toy gently up and down.

3. Have the children see how high they can bounce the soft toy without letting it fall off the parachute.

4. Hide some large, soft toys under the parachute. The children should try to guess from the shape and feel of each what it is.

5. Work together to practice wafting the parachute really high, so it catches a lot of air.

Other Ideas...

- Have the children hold the parachute at waist height and carefully roll the edges in, reducing the overall size of the parachute by about half. As they hold onto the edge of the parachute, ask them to move together toward the door, for example, on tiptoe. Have the children move forward, backward, or to different parts of the room. Use different ways of traveling while holding onto the parachute, such as shuffling on bottoms, taking giant steps, slithering on bellies, and so on.

- Have the children sit close together in two groups on opposite sides of the parachute, with their legs stretched out under the parachute. They should grip the parachute firmly and rock backward and forward in a rowing action, singing "Row, Row, Row Your Boat, Gently Down the Stream."

Shake It Fast and Shake It Slowly

Seasonal cutouts rain down on children after they lift them into the air with the parachute.

What You Need

- construction paper
- scissors
- markers
- parachute

Vocabulary

- count
- cutout
- edge
- fast/slow
- high
- holiday
- merry-go-round
- move
- season
- shape
- throw
- toss

What Children Learn

- To listen and respond to what they hear
- To interact with others and work together toward a common goal
- To associate certain shapes with a holiday or a season

What to Do

1. Make holiday or seasonal cutouts. For example, cut out snowflakes for winter, tissue paper ghosts and black paper bats for Halloween, autumn leaves, stars, hearts, shamrocks, and so on.

2. Ask the children to stand or sit around the outside edge of the flat parachute.

3. Distribute a few cutouts to each child. Ask the children to toss their cutouts onto the parachute.

4. Have the children move lots of different ways with the parachute. For example:
   - Shake the parachute fast and then slowly.
   - Lift the parachute up high on the count of three to toss the cutouts into the air.

- Hold the parachute in one hand and walk in a circle like a merry-go-round, lifting the parachute up and down gently.

5. After making the cutouts go into the air, some may fall onto the floor around the parachute. The children may pick up the items that fall near them and throw them back into the parachute.

Other Ideas ...

- Toss the cutouts under the parachute and call on one or two children at a time to go under and pick up the items while the others hold the parachute up high. For example: *Tanya and Jose, go under the parachute and pick up just one star;* or *find two stars;* or *pick up as many as you can.* If you are using colored leaves, ask the children to go under the parachute and find *just one red leaf* or *just the yellow leaves*.

- Some parachutes have a hole in the middle of them. If your parachute has a hole, challenge the children to gently shake the parachute until all the cutouts fall through the hole.

Index by Learning Objective

What Children Learn

Index by Learning Objective   83

Index

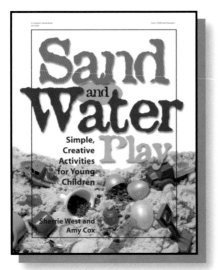

Creative new ways to help children
learn and discover with 70 sand and
water table activities.
ISBN 978-0-87659-247-2
Gryphon House / 16281 / PB

Children learn to play instruments
along with their favorite songs with
this fun activity book!
ISBN 978-0-87659-290-8
Gryphon House / 15445 / PB

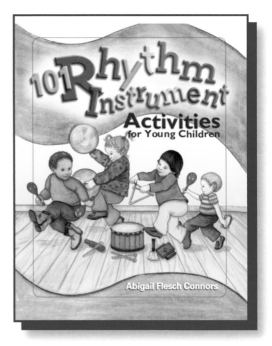

Create craft-board trees, railroad
tracks, and skyscrapers, and discover
children's joy of learning through
block play.
ISBN 978-0-87659-253-3
Gryphon House / 19327 / PB

New and classic games—each
with a non-competitive twist—
get children up and moving!
ISBN 978-0-87659-006-5
Gryphon House / 11308 / PB

More than 200 activities that
encourage children to explore
their world through open-ended
art experiences.
ISBN 978-0-87659-168-0
Gryphon House / 16985 / PB

Children learn to predict
outcomes, ask questions, and
investigate answers with 250
science activities.
ISBN 978-0-87659-272-4
Gryphon House / 12891 / PB

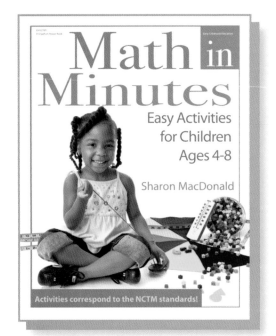

Children go on a geometric shape hunt, measure with pompoms, and find missing numbers with *Math in Minutes*.
ISBN 978-0-87659-057-7
Gryphon House / 12795 / PB

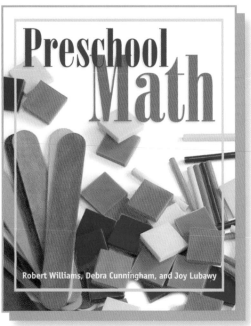

Preschool Math introduces math concepts that build foundations for a lifetime of learning and encourage wondering and exploration.
ISBN 978-0-87659-000-3
Gryphon House / 12753 / PB

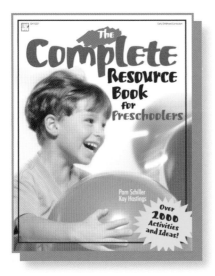

The perfect planning guide
and resource for responding
to children's interests.
ISBN 978-0-87659-195-6
Gryphon House / 15327 / PB

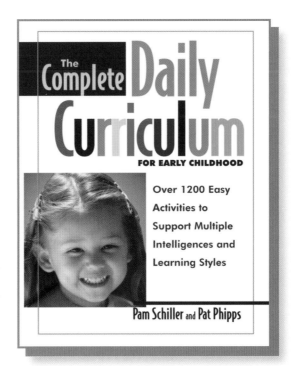

This innovative book
for children 3-6 years old
offers complete plans for
every learning style.
ISBN 978-0-87659-228-1
Gryphon House / 16279 / PB

Each of the more than 600 activities, stories, games, recipes, props, and dances in this resource enhances any curriculum!
ISBN 978-0-87659-280-9
Gryphon House / 16284 / PB

With more than 600 circle and group time activities covering 48 themes, this book is jam-packed with ideas teachers love.
ISBN 978-0-87659-181-9
Gryphon House / 16413 / PB

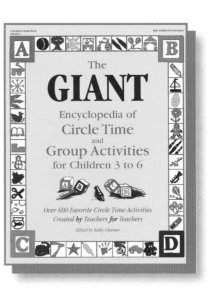

The 700 rhymes, songs, poems, fingerplays, and chants will help children learn rhythm, rhyme, and repetition, which are building blocks of literacy.
ISBN 978-0-87659-267-0
Gryphon House / 18264 / PB

Imaginative curriculum-spanning ideas
for science, math, art, and music, as well
as for cooking and holidays.
ISBN 978-0-87659-012-6
Gryphon House / 15002 / PB

More than 600 classroom-tested
activities that engage children's
imaginations and provide months of
learning fun.
ISBN 978-0-87659-166-6
Gryphon House / 19216 / PB

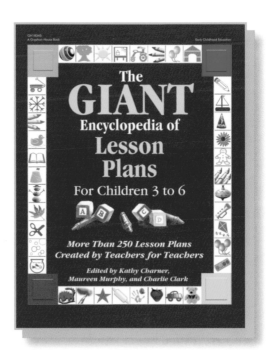

More than 250 complete lesson plans,
with topics ranging from colors to
seasons to nursery rhymes.
ISBN 978-0-87659-068-3
Gryphon House / 18345 / PB